# Unlocking the Origins of Blockchain Tech

## *From Ciphers to Cryptocurrency*

# Table of Contents

# Chapter 1. Introduction

In this illuminating Special Report, we invite you on a fascinating journey that decrypts the complex origins of Blockchain technology, methodically tracing it from its rudimentary ciphers to the groundbreaking creation of cryptocurrency. This chronicle isn't just for the tech-savvy; it is designed to guide readers of all backgrounds through the labyrinth of cryptographic technology with an approachable and engaging narrative. Understand the origins and revolutionary potential of this game-changing innovation, and see how it's transforming not just finance but entire societal structures. This vibrant report is packed with insights sure to intrigue even the casually curious. Uncover the mysteries of Blockchain technology and see the future it's shaping—step inside, and let's explore together.

# Chapter 2. Decoding Blockchain: The Basics

Like the first light after a long night, Blockchain emerged in 2008, bringing forth one of the most profound technological revolutions of the 21st century. Its origins, deeply embedded in mathematical and cryptographic concepts, provide an indelible story, a pathway from rudimentary ciphers to the groundbreaking creation of cryptocurrency. Before diving into the origins and revolutionary potential of Blockchain, we first must comprehend what it is and how it operates.

## 2.1. Defining Blockchain

In the simplest of terms, a Blockchain is a type of database. Databases are structured collections of data. These data points exist in records, which are further organized in tables to help search, filter, or manipulate them. The key difference lies in the way data is structured and stored. Traditional databases use a "table" format to organize data, while a Blockchain stores data in units called "blocks" that are then chained together.

When a block is filled with data, it's chained onto the previous block, forming a chain of blocks collectively known as - you guessed it right - Blockchain. Hence, any changes made in one block would mean recomputing all following blocks, making irrevocable changes blatantly obvious. This ingenious setup enables unparalleled security and transparency in transactions.

## 2.2. The Essence of Decentralization

One central notion behind Blockchain is "decentralization." In traditional transactions, we rely on centralized institutions, such as banks or government bodies, entrusted to facilitate transactions and store records accurately. This offers efficiency but comes with drawbacks. The system could crumble if these authorities act dishonestly or are compromised.

Blockchain technology presents a radical solution - decentralization. Transactions happen over a network of computers, termed "nodes," with no need for a central authority. Each node possesses a complete copy of the entire Blockchain, constantly updated with new blocks of transactions. If one node is compromised, the others persist, maintaining the integrity of the Blockchain. This removes single points of failure and makes it resilient against dishonest players.

## 2.3. Safety Through Cryptography

Cryptography is the spine of Blockchain and ensures its security. Each block in a Blockchain contains data and two important types of cryptographic elements: a hash and the hash of the previous block. A hash is a unique string of characters produced by a hash function, which takes an input and returns a fixed size string of bytes. Any small change in input drastically changes the output, making the process irreversible.

The inclusion of the previous block's hash effectively interlinks the blocks. An attempt to alter a block's content necessitates a change in the hash, which impacts all succeeding blocks. With the tremendous computing power required for such a recalculation, illicit changes are practically impossible without being noticed.

## 2.4. The Peer-to-Peer Network

Central to the functionality of Blockchain is the peer-to-peer network. This is a network where tasks and workloads are partitioned among peers, with no central coordination by servers. In this case, the nodes or 'peers' have the same privileges and communication capabilities.

Participants, often known as "miners," keep the network alive, and together, they verify and record transactions to the Blockchain.

To maintain consensus, all nodes follow a 'consensus protocol' to agree on the Blockchain's status. The earliest and arguably most widely adopted protocol is Bitcoin's Proof of Work. Here, the first miner to solve a mathematical puzzle gets the privilege to add a new block to the Blockchain, incentivized with a cryptocurrency reward. However, this protocol is energy-intensive, prompting the development and adoption of greener alternatives like Proof of Stake and Delegated Proof of Stake.

## 2.5. The Birth of Cryptocurrency

The first application of Blockchain was Bitcoin, a digital currency that disrupted the financial markets. Created by an anonymous figure or group known as Satoshi Nakamoto, Bitcoin spearheaded the world's engagement with Blockchain technology and opened new frontiers of possibilities.

Cryptocurrencies like Bitcoin work on the same principles mentioned above. Transactions are added to the blocks, encrypted, and linked to the previous block's hash. Miners verify transactions, add new blocks, and get rewarded with tokens of that cryptocurrency. With no need for an intermediary, these digital assets promise increased financial autonomy and offer an alternative to traditional currencies issued by central banks.

In conclusion, the Blockchain is a revolutionary technology that provides a secure, transparent, decentralized, and smooth method for recording transactions and transferring assets. It was developed out of a need for a disintermediated, trustworthy, and publicly accessible ledger. The invention of Bitcoin widened the horizon of what's possible with this technology. Despite its tech-heavy operation, the principle behind it is straightforward, user-centric, and targeted to foster an open, distributed world. The success of Bitcoin and its underlying technology represents the first steps in a revolution with potential applications far beyond cryptocurrencies.

# Chapter 3. Cryptographic Ciphers: The Ancestors of Blockchain

Before we delve into blockchain technology and its multifarious applications today, it is crucial to take a time-traveled stroll through the progenitors of this phenomenon – cryptographic ciphers. Ciphers, the clandestine machines of cryptography, laid the groundwork for the advanced cryptographic techniques prevalent in blockchain.

## 3.1. The Genesis of Cryptography

Cryptography, the science of secret coding and decoding, traces its roots back to ancient times. It was a pivotal tool during wartime, cloaking sensitive information from enemies, and in peaceful periods, preserving sacred and political secrets. The earliest form of cryptography, substitution ciphers, involved simple letters or symbol substitutions. Among these was the Caesar cipher, used by Roman Emperor Julius Caesar around 58 BC to veil his military communications.

## 3.2. Substitution Ciphers: An Inception

Substitution ciphers function by systematically replacing each element (such as a letter) in the plaintext (original message) to generate a ciphertext (scrambled message). In the Caesar cipher, for instance, a shift of three places would replace 'A' with 'D', 'B' with 'E', and so on. It provided a rudimentary layer of protection, easily deciphered if the system was understood. But during the Roman epoch, this was sufficient to secure intelligence against threats.

# 3.3. Progression to Advanced Ciphers

Substitution ciphers evolved into advanced versions with the advent of Polyalphabetic Substitution Ciphers, a notable example being the Vigenère cipher. To enhance security, Vigenère employed different Caesar ciphers based on a letter of a keyword. It represents an early attempt at introducing key-based security, adding an exceptional layer of complexity compared to its Caesar counterpart.

# 3.4. Transposition Ciphers: Shuffling Secrets

Another pivotal player in the evolution of cryptography is the transposition cipher. Unlike substitution counterparts, transposition ciphers do not substitute characters but reshuffle the order in plaintext. A simple example is the Rail Fence cipher, where text is written in a zigzag pattern across two or more lines and the encrypted cipher results from reading along the lines.

## 3.4.1. Columnar Transposition Cipher

One sophisticated instance of transposition ciphers is the Columnar Transposition Cipher. It writes the plaintext into rows of a predetermined fixed length, then scrambles it by permuting the columns. Upon reading line-by-line, the result is an intricately jumbled piece of encrypted intelligence.

# 3.5. Codebreakers: Exploiting Cipher Weakness

Albeit revolutionary for their time, even advanced ciphers were vulnerable, as codebreakers learned to exploit patterns in the ciphertext. This led to frequency analysis—exploiting the recurring usage of certain letters—and other decryption techniques that could unravel secrets behind the most judicious ciphers. Such weaknesses obviated the need for randomized encryption to blur common patterns, leading to the creation of the One-Time Pad.

## 3.6. The One-Time Pad: A Perfect Cipher?

The One-Time Pad (OTP), accredited to be theoretically uncrackable, utilized a random key as long as the message, used only once. Each character from the plaintext is encrypted by a character from the secret random key, generating the final ciphertext. However, the question of secure key distribution remained – a challenge inherited by modern cryptography.

## 3.7. Modern Cryptography: A Quantum Leap

Fast-tracking to the era of computers and digitization, cryptography took a massive stride forward. With the development of algorithms that use binary codes to encrypt and decrypt messages, communications became even more secure. Symmetric key cryptography (like AES) and asymmetric key cryptography (like RSA), along with hash functions, have built the fortifications of today's data security.

## 3.8. Cryptography and Blockchain: The Connection

From substitution to transposition, from OTP to RSA, each milestone in cryptography serves as stepping stones leading to the invention of blockchain. Blockchain applies these age-old principles combined with advanced cryptographic functions—digital signatures, hash functions, and the 'zero-knowledge proof'—to secure transactions and data. Moreover, blockchain's decentralized structure leverages these cryptographic features, promising near-impervious security against many traditional forms of cyber attacks.

Ultimately, walking through the lineage of ciphers unveils the essence of cryptocurrencies and the expansive potential of blockchain technology. It underscores how fundamental cryptographic ciphers, albeit primitive, were instrumental in paving the pathway for the revolution in digital security we associate with blockchain technology today. As we grow to understand and appreciate this complex landscape, we come one step closer to deciphering the encrypted future ahead.

# Chapter 4. Unraveling Cryptography: The Pillar of Blockchain

The discovery of cryptography, the science of encoding and decoding information, has played a critical role in various forms of communication, power balances, and, more recently, in digital finance. Most importantly, it has become the backbone of any blockchain technology.

==="The Birth of Cryptography"

Cryptography was born almost 4000 years ago in the fertile crescent of Mesopotamia, modern-day Iraq, where scribes veiled their clay-tablet messages in private language. Over the centuries, cryptography evolved dramatically. In World War II, for instance, code-breakers in Europe and Asia effected the tides of war by decoding Axis powers' encrypted transmissions. However, the moment of seismic change in the cryptographic landscape was the emergence of the digital era.

In the digital age, cryptography has expanded beyond military and diplomatic use, playing a crucial role in protecting information transmitted through digital networks. It helps in guarding against theft, tampering, or spying on sensitive data. At the heart of modern cryptography is the algorithm - a set of mathematical instructions used to transform plaintext into ciphertext and back again. One form, known as symmetric-key cryptography, involves the use of a single key for both encryption and decryption. Asymmetric-key systems introduce multiple keys: at least one public key for encryption and one private key for decryption.

==="Symmetric vs. Asymmetric Cryptography"

Symmetric-key cryptography is straightforward. The sender and receiver agree on a secret key and use it for encrypting and decrypting all messages. The drawback is that if the key is compromised, all communication becomes vulnerable. The symmetric technique led to the creation of the famous Data Encryption Standard (DES) and its successor, the Advanced Encryption Standard (AES).

In contrast, asymmetric cryptography, or public-key cryptography, uses two keys. Imagine a mailbox with a slot and a lock. Anyone can drop a letter (public key) in the slot, but only the owner, with the corresponding private key, can open the mailbox to read the message. A famous example is the RSA algorithm — named after its creators, Ron Rivest, Adi Shamir, and Leonard Adleman.

==="The Heart of Blockchain: Cryptographic Hash Functions"

In understanding blockchain, one cannot overlook the critical concept of cryptographic hash functions. They are a type of algorithm that takes an input (or 'message') and returns a fixed-size string of bytes. The output, or "hash," is unique to each unique input. A minute change in input will produce such a drastically different output that the new hash appears uncorrelated with the old hash. Two critical features make hashes secure for encoding transactions on a blockchain: they are deterministic, and they offer high collision resistance.

To explain, a hash function is deterministic, meaning that the same input will always produce the same output. In the world of cryptography, this deterministic nature is fundamental. Secondly, the hash functions are designed to be collision-resistant. That is, it is extremely unlikely (but not impossible) that two different inputs will produce the same hash output. This characteristic is crucial in preventing fraudulent manipulation of blockchain transactions.

==="Adding Timestamps and Transactions to the Mix"

Now that we have an understanding of modern cryptography and the role of hashes let's explore how these concepts are woven into the fabric of blockchain. In the most simple terms, a block in a blockchain contains data (frequently a list of transactions), a timestamp, and the cryptographic hash of the previous block in the chain.

When a block is added to the chain, it's connected to the previous block via the cryptographic hash. Consider these hashes as the "glue" that holds the blockchain together. If someone attempts to alter the data within a block, the hash of the block changes, but the next block in the chain still contains the old hash. This mismatch reveals the tampering, ensuring the data in blocks are immutable, a cornerstone of blockchain security.

==="Cryptocurrencies: Blockchain's Flagship Application"

The most famous application of blockchain technology to date is cryptocurrency, the first of which was Bitcoin. Satoshi Nakamoto, Bitcoin's pseudonymous creator, combined existing cryptographic protocols in a groundbreaking way to create the Bitcoin protocol.

Each Bitcoin transaction is securely signed with the sender's private key, proving that the sender owns the Bitcoins being transferred. These transactions are then validated by other nodes in the network (known as miners) and added to a public, immutable ledger — the blockchain. Each miner then works on confirming a new block filled with transactions by solving a complex mathematical problem, a process known as proof-of-work.

Blockchain technology and modern cryptography have set the stage for peer-to-peer digital currencies, offering security, privacy, and freedom from central authority. Beyond cryptocurrencies, the applications for the blockchain are vast and multifaceted, from supply chain oversight to voting systems, hinting at a future filled with exciting possibilities.

==="Future Prospects and Challenges"

As we look towards the horizon, it's apparent that blockchain technology, underpinned by the principles of cryptography, offers tremendous potential for revolutionizing a variety of industries. It promises a world where transactions and data are secure, trustless, and decentralized. However, like any transformative technology, it also presents its own unique challenges and hurdles. There are concerns surrounding scalability, energy consumption, interoperability between different blockchains, and, notably, the need for a robust legal framework addressing blockchain's implications.

In conclusion, the remarkable journey of cryptography, from simple ciphers to becoming an integral part of the digital era — powering not just blockchain but helping secure our digital world — is a testament to human ingenuity. Its complexities may be daunting, but with careful study, the layers peel back to reveal a structure that, while intricate, is both fascinating and revolutionary. As blockchain continues to develop and adapt, the ciphers and codes that have given rise to this technology will continue to keep the digital world secure and open new doors for innovation.

# Chapter 5. Bitcoin: The Spark that Ignited the Blockchain Revolution

As we shift into the new age of digital technology, a very distinct trailblazer chose to make itself known in the form of Bitcoin, a novel class of digital money leveraging the power of blockchain technology to achieve decentralization, privacy, and security.

## 5.1. The Genesis of Bitcoin

Bitcoin was created by an anonymous entity or entities going by the name Satoshi Nakamoto, who released the Bitcoin whitepaper in late 2008, potentially in response to the financial crisis that year. Though shrouded in mystery, the objective was clear: to create a decentralized currency free from control by any single entity and protected from manipulation.

Bitcoin was designed as a peer-to-peer system, wherein transactions are performed directly between the parties involved, without the need for intermediaries. This was a radical departure from traditional financial systems, where banks or financial institutions often function as the middlemen in all transactions.

## 5.2. The Underlying Mechanics

Underpinning Bitcoin is the proof-of-work (PoW) consensus mechanism within its blockchain structure. When a transaction is performed, it needs to be verified and added to the 'block,' a process handled by bitcoin miners. Miners utilize significant computational resources to resolve complex mathematical problems, and the first to resolve the problem gets the right to add the new block to the blockchain, receiving a certain number of bitcoins as a reward.

This consensus mechanism achieves two primary purposes: it ensures the validity of transactions and further distributes new bitcoins into the system without the need for a central authority. In essence, it upholds the basic principles of decentralization.

# 5.3. Disruptive Potential and Limitations

Bitcoin's disruptive potential primarily lies in its decentralization. It provides a democratic system where every participant has equal power, breaking from the conventional financial system where power is concentrated among a few major players. This allows for a truly global financial system where anyone can participate, without being limited by borders or controlled by central authorities.

However, it's essential to highlight some limitations. For one, Bitcoin's mining process, due to its intensive computational nature, consumes a significant amount of energy. Furthermore, while Bitcoin transactions are pseudonymous, they are also publicly accessible, leading to potential privacy concerns. And finally, the price volatility of Bitcoin raises questions about its reliability as a stable store of value.

# 5.4. Bitcoin: More Than Just Digital Gold

Despite its downsides, Bitcoin has managed to carve out a unique spot in the financial world. The built-in scarcity of Bitcoin - capped at 21 million Bitcoins - coupled with its decentralized nature has earned it the nickname "digital gold."

It serves as an alternative investment for diversifying portfolios, an instrument to hedge against traditional financial markets, and in some cases, even as a protest against systems deemed corrupt or unfair.

Bitcoin's influence extends beyond financial applications. Its underlying technology - the blockchain - has opened the doors for a variety of non-financial applications, such as supply-chain management, identity verification, and democratic governance, amongst others.

## 5.5. Into the Future

As we look towards the future, we approach with a sense of awe and optimism. Bitcoin has already prompted numerous responses worldwide - from concern and skepticism to intrigue and fascination. While there is still significant work to be done in regulating and managing the use of such technology, it's undeniably clear that Bitcoin and its underlying blockchain technology hold the potential to revolutionize not just financial systems, but society as a whole. There may well come a day when concepts such as decentralization, blockchain, and cryptocurrency are as commonplace as the internet and smartphones.

To conclude, Bitcoin was the spark that ignited the blockchain revolution. A change catalyst propelling us into an era where financial transactions and trust can be decentralized, paving the way for numerous opportunities. As we traverse through this technological revolution, it's crucial to remember that, like all powerful tools, understanding and prudence are vital in wielding it effectively.

# Chapter 6. Understanding Cryptocurrency: More Than Digital Cash

To comprehend Cryptocurrency, one must cast aside preconceived notions about traditional finance. Unlike the coins and paper notes that fill our wallets, cryptocurrency exists entirely in a digital realm—it holds no tangible form, yet its value and impact are powerfully real.

## 6.1. Unraveling the Definition

Cryptography, an ancient method used to secure communication in the face of adversaries, is critical to the definition of cryptocurrency. Built atop a subfield of cryptography, known as Cryptology, this digital asset's core characteristics are its secure nature, decentralization, and the immutable audit trails it offers. Consequently, cryptocurrency's principal purpose is to serve as a medium of exchange within digital space, where stringent encryption techniques guarantee transactions' security and control creation of additional units.

Peer-to-peer networks—decentralized groupings of participants who share resources—are intrinsic to this operation. In this digital realm, traditional intermediaries like banks become irrelevant, with individuals gaining direct control over their finances.

## 6.2. From the Roots: Bitcoin and the Birth of Cryptocurrency

Cryptocurrency's story began with Bitcoin, conceived in 2008 by an unknown inventor known only as Satoshi Nakamoto. Nakamoto introduced a whitepaper titled 'Bitcoin: A Peer-to-Peer Electronic Cash System,' thereby laying the foundation for a new field of technology.

Bitcoin's inception during a time of financial crisis was far from accidental. In fact, the genesis block—the inaugural block mined on the Bitcoin blockchain—included the cryptic message: "The Times 03/Jan/2009 Chancellor on brink of second bailout for banks." This pointed reference underscored Bitcoin's core ethos—that of a currency free from centralized control, untethered by institutional instability.

# 6.3. Mysterious Mechanics: How does Cryptocurrency Work?

Cryptocurrency relies on encompassing technology known as Blockchain. The transactions—however big or small—are grouped in blocks, and each block is cryptographically linked to its predecessor to form a 'blockchain'. But before a block can be added, it must be validated.

This work falls to miners—participants with high computational processing power who solve complex algorithms—to judge each transaction's legitimacy. For their work, they earn transaction fees and are occasionally rewarded with new cryptocurrency—a process known as Proof of Work. This robust system creates a powerful deterrent against fraud, ensuring the integrity of transactions.

Later came the introduction of Proof of Stake—an energy-efficient alternative to Proof of Work. Rather than rewarding miners who solve algorithms, Proof of Stake privileges holder's coin age and volume, fostering a sense of long-term investment and commitment amongst participants.

# 6.4. Prominent Features of Cryptocurrency

Cryptocurrencies harbor several unique attractions that differentiate them from traditional forms of value exchange:

1. Deterministic supply: The true value of any currency lies strictly in its scarcity. This principle is embedded within cryptocurrencies like Bitcoin, where the total supply is capped at 21 million coins, thereby forestalling devaluation by inflation.

2. Pseudonymity: In contrast to conventional banking structures, cryptocurrency transactions are pseudo-anonymous. Each person can have one or many identifiers not explicitly connected to their real-world identity.

3. Irreversibility: Once a transaction is confirmed, there's no turning back—it cannot be reversed by anyone, not even network participants with the most extensive computing power. While this quality bolsters trust and integrity, it also places the onus on users to conduct transactions carefully.

4. Geographic flexibility: Cryptocurrency knows no borders; it can be sent and received anywhere worldwide, provided there's an internet connection. This makes it especially attractive in countries with unstable currencies.

# 6.5. The Fruits of Decentralization: DApps and Smart Contracts

The decentralization characteristic of cryptocurrency is not limited to finance—it extends to applications as well. Called decentralized applications, or DApps, they operate on blockchain technology—completely open-source, public, and resistant to censorship.

Smart contracts are another revolutionary offshoot of cryptocurrency. These self-executing contracts detail the obligations of involved parties, with the terms embedded into lines of code. The beauty of smart contracts lies in their autonomy—once conditions are met, they automatically execute, removing the need for a middleman and substantially reducing the risk of fraud.

# 6.6. Tomorrow's Digital Gold?

Believers champion cryptocurrency as the future of money—an evolution as seismic as the leap from barter to coinage. Skeptics, meanwhile, fear its volatility and potential for facilitating illicit activities. Yet, as we delve deeper into the 21st Century, the propagation of cryptocurrency—facilitated by surges in technological innovation and public interest—seems increasingly inevitable.

In the end, comprehending cryptocurrency leads us to a more profound intent: understanding the potentials of human ingenuity when it meets the uncharted possibilities of technology. Despite uncertainties, there's an emerging consensus that cryptocurrency, like electricity or the internet, stands as a potent invention that's destined to redefine countless aspects of our lives.

As the narrative continues to unfold, capitalizing on the opportunities and navigating the risks inherent in this vibrant, dynamic sector will call for knowledge, adaptability, and an inquisitive, open-minded spirit.

# Chapter 7. Security in Blockchain: How It Bulletproofs Transactions

Blockchain technology is widely recognized for its robust security features, which makes it an attractive option for a myriad of applications, most notably, financial transactions. This chapter aims to delve into the underlying security mechanisms in blockchain, which guarantee privacy, data integrity and prevent fraudulent activities, hence rendering transactions bulletproof.

## 7.1. The Immutable Ledger

The heart of blockchain security is the concept of immutability. In blockchain terminology, immutability refers to the unchanging nature of the data once it has been written into the blockchain. The digital ledger recording transactions in the blockchain is designed in a way that any tampering, alteration, or deletion of data is virtually impossible. On a more technical level, this is achieved through cryptographic hashes.

Every transaction or data block in a blockchain is associated with a unique cryptographic hash. This hash is derived from the transaction data itself. Even a tiny modification to the transaction data alters the hash significantly. Consequently, any attempt at modification immediately becomes evident because the hash changes, effectively alerting the system to the tampering.

However, the immutability of the blockchain does not just rely on individual block hashes. The sequence of transactions and blocks is equally important, and this is where the concept of 'blocks' and 'chains' within blockchain manifests itself. Each block contains a reference to the hash of the previous block, creating a chained sequence. This means a change in one block disrupts the sequence because the next block's reference will no longer match the altered hash. It is this interconnectedness that significantly raises the bar for any potential data tampering.

## 7.2. Encryption and Private Keys

The currency of the realm in blockchain security is encryption, typically realized through public-key cryptography. Each user in the blockchain network has a pair of cryptographic keys: a public key, which is openly available, and a private key, which is kept secret.

The public key is used by others in the network to encrypt data or validate transactions destined for or originating from the owner of that public key. The private key, on the other hand, is used to decrypt received data, sign transactions, or in more general terms, prove ownership.

A user's identity in the network is tied to their public-private key pair. This effectively prevents identity theft, provided the private key is kept secure. If Alice wants to send a message (or a transaction) to Bob, she will use Bob's public key to encrypt the data. Bob can then use his private key to decrypt this data. If Bob wants to prove to Alice that a message is genuinely from him, he can 'sign' the message using his private key. Alice can then validate the signature using Bob's public key.

## 7.3. Consensus Mechanisms

Blockchain security isn't just about preventing data tampering or ensuring transaction authenticity; it's also about maintaining the integrity of the network and preventing fraudulent behavior, such as double-spending. This is where consensus mechanisms come into play.

A consensus mechanism is a protocol that ensures all nodes participating in the network agree on the validity of transactions and the state of the blockchain. There are several consensus mechanisms, but the most well-known are Proof of Work (PoW) and Proof of Stake (PoS).

In PoW, a complex mathematical problem must be solved to create a new block. The computing power required to solve this problem is a deterrent against fraudulent activities because it is costly and time-consuming. Moreover, any attempt to alter past transactions would require re-mining all subsequent blocks — an effort that would outstrip any potential benefit.

PoS, on the other hand, chooses the creator of the new block based on their 'stake' or ownership of tokens in the blockchain. The more tokens owned, the more likely to get chosen. This way, parties with a vested interest in preserving the network's integrity are those more likely to participate in its maintenance.

## 7.4. Smart Contracts

Smart contracts are self-executing contracts with the terms of the agreement directly written into code. They are used extensively in blockchain networks to facilitate and verify transactions without third parties. These contracts are generally immutable; once deployed, they cannot be altered. This ensures that once the terms are agreed upon and encoded into the contract, neither party can renege or modify those terms.

Smart contracts also improve security through automation they eliminate manual procedures, and hence, the risk of human error. Moreover, the absence of a need for a trusted third party removes a potential point of vulnerability.

# 7.5. Conclusion: The Road Ahead for Blockchain Security

As we've walked through the mechanisms that secure blockchain transactions, from immutability and encryption to consensus protocols and smart contracts, we can see how these elements work together to form an armor around transactions, rendering them bulletproof. It is this robustness that brings trust and transparency to transactions, heralding a new way of transferring value in an increasingly digital world.

However, blockchain security continues to evolve to both tackle new threats and improve current solutions. While the blockchain itself is robust, the ecosystem build around it, including wallet software, exchange platforms, and the human element, can still be vulnerable.

Blockchain, thus, is not invincible, and there are indeed challenges that need addressing. Yet, its inherent security provisions lay down a promising foundation, opening paths to continued innovation in securing our digital future.

# Chapter 8. Blockchain Applications: Beyond Bitcoin and Financial World

While Bitcoin, an initial and most prominent product of Blockchain technology, serves as a digital gold reference — a method of transferring and storing value, it doesn't begin to tap into the broader scope where this technology can be utilized. Let's embark on an exploration of different applications, from supply chains to voting systems, illustrating blockchain's potential to revolutionize countless industries.

## 8.1. Supply Chain Management

In an increasingly globalised world, supply chains have become intricate webs of transactions. Mismanagement, unintentional mistakes, and intentional fraud all have the capacity to cause substantial loss. Blockchain provides a potential solution to these issues through increased transparency and traceability.

Each stage in a product's lifecycle could be documented on a blockchain, from raw materials to the finished product. This ledger, universally accessible and unalterable, could then be utilized to verify authenticity or fair trade status, or to prove compliance with regional laws. Blockchain's applications in supply chains extend to include tracking of rare earth minerals, 'conflict-free' diamonds, and even pedigree in livestock.

## 8.2. Health Care

In health care, there is a constant stress test between privacy and accessibility of medical records. Controlled by disparate entities, from hospitals to local GPs and private practitioners, a person's healthcare data can become fragmented and deficient. Yet, Blockchain's decentralised nature and secure encryption could enable a person's entire medical history to exist on a single secure and accessible network.

An individual could have ownership of their medical data, granting access to different parts to their medical practitioners, and could also provide access to pharmaceutical researchers anonymously, promoting the enhancement of medical treatments and strategies.

## 8.3. Voting and Democracy

Voting systems globally are often out-of-date and vulnerable to abuse. Digitizing them in the past has been challenging due to security concerns. Yet here too, Blockchain's distributed ledger with its robust safeguards can meaningfully contribute.

Existing on the blockchain ledger, each vote would become almost impossible to tamper with. Citizens can participate in the democratic process securely and transparently, having faith that votes haven't been tampered with or voters falsely disenfranchised.

## 8.4. Intellectual Property (IP) and Royalties

As we move into an increasingly digital age, protection, tracking, and monetization of Intellectual Property (IP) has become challenging. Fairly allocating royalties to artists for their work is an area where blockchain could make a significant impact.

The blockchain could serve as an indisputable registry for copyright and patent ownership, leading to less legal infrastructure and bureaucracy needed to manage IP. Artists could also directly publish their work on the blockchain, automatically setting up smart contacts to handle royalties' distribution.

# 8.5. Decentralized Energy Grids

With rising concern over sustainability and the environment, there is a need for efficient, clean energy sources. The current energy distribution model is centralized and can result in inefficiencies due to power degradation over long distances. Decentralized energy grids powered by blockchain can change this.

Energy producers could sell surplus power directly to consumers via a blockchain network. Smart meters would record usage and relay it in real-time to the blockchain, automatically conducting transactions between consumer and producer. This could revolutionize the way we consume and distribute power, leading to more sustainable and efficient energy usage.

# 8.6. Public Services

Public services such as taxation, welfare, and licensing could significantly benefit from blockchain technology. By reducing bureaucracy, minimizing inefficiency and closing avenues for corruption, it can revolutionize the way we interact with public services.

Taxation could be automatically handled via a blockchain, with transaction taxes collected at the point of sale. Welfare payments could be distributed through a similar system, making sure they go directly to the intended recipient. Licenses could be stored on an individual's profile on the blockchain, making validation quick and easy.

To conclude, it's clear to see that blockchain technology extends far beyond Bitcoin and the financial world. While we're still at the dawn of realizing blockchain's full potential, the disruptive nature of this technology promises to be a driving force in shaping our society in the coming decades. The horizon is expansive; the limits, if any, are yet unknown. Come aboard the Blockchain walk; the journey promises to be thrilling.

# Chapter 9. Potential and Challenges: The Blockchain Paradox

The dawn of the digital age has presented us with a buffet of paradoxical situations – the comforting omnipresence of technology, intertwined with the chilling reality of surveillance; the incredible feats of data storage, with the looming threats of cyber breaches. Rooted in this tangled hotbed of digital paradoxes, Blockchain technology takes center stage, catalyzing a revolution, while simultaneously facing an array of challenges that demand addressing.

## 9.1. Blockchain: An Overview

A blockchain is essentially a decentralized, distributed ledger system that securely records transactions across multiple computers. Its allure lies in its promise of trust, privacy, and security, courtesy of cryptography.

Transactions and interactions conducted on a blockchain are encrypted and stored across multiple computers, creating a chain of records. Once established, these records are highly resistant to change and manipulation, thereby offering a heightened level of security.

Blockchain's decentralized nature, in theory, allows it to thrive outside of traditional banking systems and government regulations. Consequently, it has been paving the way for a myriad of applications beyond just cryptocurrency, ranging from supply chain logistics, healthcare, land registry to even elections and governance.

However, as enticing as it may sound, blockchain is embroiled in a paradox, a seemingly contradicting state between its boundless potential and profound challenges it must rise over – the blockchain paradox.

## 9.2. The Unbounded Potential

While cryptocurrency is the most well-known application of blockchain, the technology's potential reaches far beyond. Blockchain's inherent decentralization, transparency, data integrity, and robustness form an impressive backbone for a remarkable range of applications.

In supply chain management, blockchain can offer real-time visibility into goods being transported, their origins, and their condition. This can potentially thwart counterfeit goods, illegal activities, and enhance compliance, drastically improving quality control and trust within the market.

Governments and institutions are exploring blockchain for secure, tamper-proof voting systems. The transparency and security that blockchain brings could eliminate concerns regarding voter fraud and ensure fair, open elections all over the world.

In the field of healthcare, blockchain could revolutionize patient data management, by providing a secure and immutable record of one's medical history. This could potentially speed up diagnoses, prevent miscommunications and errors, and streamline treatments.

Yet, as exalting as these prospects are, it is essential to view them against the backdrop of the formidable challenges that blockchain faces, the other side of the paradox.

## 9.3. Navigating the Choppy Waters

While blockchain shows promise, its road to mainstream adoption is littered with obstacles, some inherent to its design, and others dictated by the society in which it operates.

Blockchain's decentralized nature, while an asset, is also a liability. It sidelines central authority, making regulatory oversight difficult. This makes it a potential harbor for illegal activities such as money laundering and fraud, especially within the context of cryptocurrency. This tricky legal area is a hurdle the technology has to clear to gain greater acceptance.

Another challenge lies in the realm of security. While blockchains are designed to be secure, they are not invulnerable. From 51% attacks, where a user gains control of the majority of network mining power, to smart contract bugs, the technology isn't without its vulnerabilities.

Data privacy, while a promise, is also a challenge. Considering anybody on the network can view the transactions, the implementation of privacy norms and regulation on such a decentralized and transparent system is complex.

Finally, the environmental impact of blockchain, particularly as seen with Bitcoin's energy use, is another pressing challenge. The proof-of-work consensus mechanism—a foundational layer for blockchain architecture—requires substantial computational power, equivalent to consuming large amounts of energy.

# 9.4. The Necessary Balancing Act

In the end, the blockchain paradox is about finding a balance between the potential and the challenges. It's about harnessing the capabilities of the technology, while taking steps to mitigate its risks. It's about embracing the potential for a decentralized future, while addressing regulatory, security, privacy, and environmental concerns.

Governments, organizations, and individuals need to work together to set standards for blockchain use, develop methods to oversee its functioning without undermining its decentralized nature, foster transparency without compromising privacy, and strive towards more energy-efficient consensus mechanisms.

In its current state, the blockchain may seem paradoxical—an entity of colossal potential in the midst of grave challenges. But paradoxes are often the starting points of innovations. The potential of blockchain technology may seem unfathomable and the path, riddled with roadblocks; it is up to us—technologists, policymakers, and users—to untangle the paradox and pave the way to the future, a future woven with blockchain. As we continue on this remarkable journey, the limits of our intellect and creativity are the only boundaries to blockchain's potential application and resolution of its accompanying challenges.

# Chapter 10. Future Predictions: The Evolution of Blockchain and Cryptocurrency

The nature of prophecy is inherently shaky, particularly in the ever-evolving world of technology. However, educated predictions on the future of blockchain technology and cryptocurrencies can be made through careful analysis of market trends, technological innovation specifics, and global economic factors.

## 10.1. The Blockchain: Beyond Cryptocurrency

Blockchain rose to prominence as the underpinning tech of Bitcoin, the first cryptocurrency. However, it's become increasingly evident that the technology is so much more than just an instrument for digital currencies. Its unique qualities — security, decentralization, transparency, and immutability — could have far-reaching ramifications in various sectors.

The beauty of blockchain is its peer-to-peer decentralized network, which implies that all transactions are instantly transparent to all participants while making third-party mediation redundant. In a time where faith in traditional financial institutions is dwindling, and concerns regarding privacy are at an all-time high, blockchain's virtues become further underscored.

Consider the healthcare industry, where patient data security is a significant issue. A blockchain-based system could securely store patient records, enabling standardized and secure access for authorized healthcare providers. This eradicates errors and lapses in information transfer among different providers and insurance companies, essentially improving patient care quality.

Another application could be the supply chain. Blockchain technology implementation can revolutionize supply chain management by providing end-to-end transparency, thereby reducing time delays, added costs, and human error that plague the current system. It will be here, in the sectorial adaptation of the technology, that blockchain's broader potential will manifest itself.

## 10.2. Next Phase in Cryptocurrency Evolution

Cryptocurrencies, the nascent financial instruments, have been amassing significant attention. Bitcoin, Ethereum, and other digital currencies have challenged conventional finance paradigms, offering a form of money that is both borderless and, theoretically, less susceptible to systemic risks.

Simultaneously, the so-termed 'Bitcoin Bubble' controversy has sparked fierce debate over cryptocurrencies' stability and longevity. To counter these risks, the concept of stablecoins emerged— cryptocurrencies tied to stable assets, like traditional fiat currencies or gold. The goal is to offer the best of both worlds: blockchain's security and decentralization with traditional finance's stability.

Looking forward, we can expect cryptocurrencies to mature, a development marked by increased stability, wider acceptance, and more standardized regulations. Blockchain's wider adaptation will undoubtedly play a role in making cryptocurrencies more mainstream.

# 10.3. The Emergence of Central Bank Digital Currency (CBDC)

Another sophisticated evolution in the global finance sector fuelled by blockchain technology is the probable inception of Central Bank Digital Currencies (CBDCs). Several countries' central banks are exploring the idea of launching their digital money. These aren't cryptocurrencies in the traditional sense, but they leverage blockchain's robustness in recording transactions and maintaining account balances.

The Chinese government, for instance, has conducted extensive beta-testing of its digital yuan, signaling its intention to lead the CBDC race. Introducing CBDCs globally could profoundly alter how global economic systems function, and how monetary policy is executed. These currencies could increase financial access in developing countries and streamline existing financial infrastructure in developed nations.

# 10.4. Implementations in Decentralized Finance (DeFi)

As we inch closer to a decentralized future, we're likely to witness a surge in the adoption of decentralized finance or DeFi — that is, the use of blockchain, cryptocurrencies, smart contracts, and more to recreate and improve upon existing financial systems.

DeFi systems could democratize finance by introducing permissionless financial systems and reducing institutional control over individual wealth. The rise in platforms offering services like lending, insurance, and even derivative trading in a decentralized environment is a definite sign of a more inclusive financial landscape powered by blockchain.

# 10.5. The Age of Interoperability

Blockchain's future will also likely be characterized by a shift towards interoperability, the ability for different blockchain networks to communicate and transact with each other seamlessly. This cross-chain integration within blockchains will enable a more connected ecosystem, driving forward the vision of blockchain as the 'Internet of Value.' It present potentials in cohesively linking all sectors, including finance, healthcare, supply chain, entertainment, and more.

The journey we embarked upon decades ago with rudimentary ciphers has brought us to a precipice of a game-changing epoch. The future of blockchain technology and cryptocurrencies is rife with possibilities that extend beyond what we can foresee today. With every passing day, the labyrinth of cryptographic technology unfurls bit by bit, nudging us closer towards an envisioned world teeming with decentralization, transparency, and unparalleled security. As suggested by this comprehensive exploration, blockchain and cryptocurrencies are not mere tech trends. Instead, they may well be shaping blocks of our societal structures in the years to come.

# Chapter 11. Blockchain: Closing Thoughts on Its Past, Present, and Future

As we approach the conclusion of our informative saga through the annals of Blockchain, we must acknowledge, understand, and duly appreciate the significant footprints which this technology has imprinted over time. The momentum and transformative power of Blockchain technology tighten their grip on a multitude of industries. With sophistication, precision, and staggering growth, Blockchain stands tall, looking back at the peaks it's conquered, reaching ambitiously towards the horizons it craves to explore.

## 11.1. The Subtle Genesis

It is crucial to revisit the humble beginnings of cryptographic technology, a critical factor that aided the evolution of Blockchain. Even the brightest ideas often have simple roots; Blockchain was not an exception. The backstory begins in the early 1990s, a time when J.R. Whitfield presented the first workable vision for a cryptographically protected chain of blocks. However, his visionary concept struggled to cast its light over the vast sea of technological development, and hence remained a theory.

The advent of the new millennium rekindled these nearly-lost sparks. Incorporating Whitfield's theoretical frame, Stuart Haber and W. Scott Stornetta developed a cryptographically secured chain of blocks, reporting hash functionalities along with time-stamping capabilities— a revelation that would lay the bedrock for our modern Blockchain.

## 11.2. An Anonymous Catalyst

Ascend now to the next base camp: 2008. A mysterious entity, Satoshi Nakamoto, brought forth a digital or, indeed, a virtual currency named Bitcoin. Engraved in its heart was the pulse of Blockchain technology. The tremors felt from this singular creation were seismic: Here was a solution promising secure, decentralized transactions—an alternative to existing dominantly centralized financial structures. Satoshi's brainchild held hands with radical pragmatism, delivering a stronger tenet of decentralization, privacy, and security.

## 11.3. The Dawn of the Disrupter

Blockchain went live with the birth of Bitcoin. The proverbial genie was out of the bottle, displaying its prowess and widening the eyes of the technology community. The disruptive power flowed with every Bitcoin transaction. In just a few years, the world recognized the tech not as Bitcoin's shadow but as an entity carrying its autonomous energy.

Blockchain started positioning itself as a significant enabler of business transformations, transcending the boundaries of financial transactions and funnelling opportunities into sectors like supply chain, logistics, voting systems, real estates, and anything else that values traceability, transparency, and trust.

## 11.4. A Spectrum of Challenges

However, as we step further into this ciphered network's depths, we encounter disarray and contradictions. The liberating capacities of Blockchain technology also confront a spectrum of regulatory, institutional, and technical challenges. Regulatory bodies grapple with understanding this technology and its broader implications.

Institutions, deeply rooted in old traditions, face turmoil embracing this new paradigm due to legacy systems. Technically, its immutable nature raises queries for data protection rights, while scalability is a concern that lingers.

## 11.5. The Galloping Present

Despite these challenges, the essence of this decentralized technology gains momentum, surges across industries, and spurred the development of a multitude of blockchains both public and private, including Ethereum, Ripple, and Hyperledger. We see the technological landscape virtually teeming with applications—smart contracts, decentralized applications, to name a few— underpinned by Blockchain. Yes, it continues to usher in an era of decentralized consensus, squeezing out inefficiencies and opening doors to possibilities hitherto undreamed.

## 11.6. Gazing into the Future

As we stand in the cusp of this futurist landscape, the prospects appear virtually untapped. Blockchain positions itself as an antidote for gigantic systems vulnerable to fraud, inefficiency, and opacity. This technology can potentially catalyze the creation of models that spur innovation, create value, and empower individuals.

While the impact on established industries is already becoming apparent, that imprint becomes bolder and more profound as we forge on. The idea of a 'Web 3.0', 'Internet of Value', or 'Trust Protocol' — a decentralized internet where wealth, assets, and even more abstract constructs like reputation can be shared and transacted without intermediaries — hover tantalizingly within reach.

In closing, it is impossible not to marvel at the ever-oblique trajectory of technological innovation. In an expanse barely spanning a couple of decades, Blockchain has sped from surprising conception, through laborious gestation and precarious birth, into precarious youth. It now stands — poised, proud, on the cusp of adulthood, scanning with bright eyes an horizon filled with unrivaled opportunities and unseen challenges.

Blockchain has shown the world a flash of its potential — and the world is hardly likely to forget it. It has made a deep and indelible impact, a pioneering innovation that portends a future of untold possibilities. The journey of blockchain from the past to the present, and into the uncertain future, unfurls an inspiring chronicle of discovery, tenacity, and transformative power— a story that we've only just begun to tell.

* 9 7 9 8 8 5 6 5 1 9 2 3 4 *